Be Proactive, Not Reactive:

Your Guide to Navigating Life's Unexpected Moments with Clarity and Confidence

Maria S. Turner

First Printing Edition 2025.
Publisher: Midlife Miracle Publishing
Las Vegas, Nevada
Cover & Layout Designer: Arnab Bhuiya
Editor: Julie Helliwell

Library of Congress Control Number: 2025910997

ISBN: 979-8-218-69584-2

For information on bulk purchases or corporate premium sales, please email contact@mariasturner.com.

Disclaimer: This book covers only United States (U.S.) procedures, processes, and laws, unless it specifically states otherwise.

The content provided is for educational purposes only and is not intended as a substitute for professional advice. It does not constitute legal, medical, financial, or mental health advice. Readers should always consult a qualified professional for guidance tailored to their specific circumstances. The author and publisher disclaim any responsibility for outcomes arising from the use of this material or for the content of any external links. While reasonable efforts have been made to ensure accuracy, please note that laws, policies, and external websites are subject to change.

Contents

Why I Wrote This Book

This book was born from a simple but powerful intention: to take the personal, behind-the-scenes conversations I've had with individuals, and offer their insights, challenges, and breakthroughs to the collective, knowing that what helps one can help many. If the people in my immediate circles—whether professional, personal, or social—were facing certain challenges, I knew they weren't alone. Others were navigating the same situations silently, often without guidance or support.

This book is my way of sharing the wisdom and insight I've gathered from over 17 years of experience working in corporate Human Resources, along with real-life crisis scenarios that my colleagues, clients, and loved ones confided in me. When they didn't know where to start, they turned to me. I listened without judgment, asked thoughtful questions, and reached out to my trusted network of attorneys, paralegals, social workers, and other professionals—experts in their fields—to help them find the best path forward. I took notes, followed up, and made sure they had what they needed to make informed decisions and move ahead with confidence.

That's the heart of this book. It's not meant to be read once and tucked away. It's designed to walk you through the many seasons of life, because life isn't linear, and most major events don't happen just once. Think about how many funerals we attend in a lifetime. Whether through family, work, or community, loss touches us again and again. Someone will always need guidance on what to do next.

Not everyone will face a medical emergency or become suddenly incapacitated, but if it does happen, wouldn't it feel better to already have a hospital plan and ICE (In Case of Emergency) protocol in place? Being proactive protects you from unnecessary stress, confusion, and emotional overwhelm. It's not about fear; it's about foresight.

When you're prepared, you can meet life's unexpected moments with clarity and calm, not because the situation is easy, but because you've already built the systems you need to respond with strength. You're not scrambling; you're activating.

Every chapter in this book is rooted in real stories—lived experiences that were shared with me in confidence by people who trusted me to help them find answers. This isn't theory. It's practical, compassionate, and wisdom shaped by real life.

And that's why I wrote this book. What was once shared in private conversations is now available to anyone ready to receive it. I've come to realize that my knowledge, experience, and insight aren't just for me or my immediate circle. They're meant to serve many.

This book is my gift to the collective—a reflection of my passion to help, guide, and make challenging moments just a little bit easier for you.

Introduction

Who This Book Is For

This book is for the person who wants to be empowered and equipped to make informed decisions but isn't sure where to start, and for anyone open to learning practical steps to navigate life's unexpected moments with clarity and confidence.

Wherever you're beginning from, you'll find clear, compassionate guidance to support you, one step at a time.

It's for you if:

- You're the person others turn to in a crisis because you stay ready, not reactive.
- You're a caregiver, advocate, or quiet leader helping hold your family together.
- You're single or child-free and want a clear, dignified plan for yourself.
- You're a first-generation wealth builder protecting the legacy you're creating.
- You manage a household, balancing emotional, financial, and everyday responsibilities.
- You or a loved one serve in the military, law enforcement, or other service-related roles where sudden deployments, relocations, or emergencies are part of life.
- You come from a community where planning wasn't always modeled, and you're determined to set a new standard.

This book also supports professionals who walk alongside families during vulnerable times: social workers, case managers, nonprofit leaders, ministry teams, funeral service providers, hospice workers, estate planners, attorneys, and financial advisors.

If you value dignity, emotional awareness, self-reliance, and clarity—
and if you believe preparation is an act of love, not fear—this book
was written for you.

You don't need to have it all figured out.
You only need the willingness to begin.
This book will walk with you, one empowered step at a time.

Why This Matters Now More Than Ever

Life often catches us off guard, sometimes with beautiful surprises,
but often with challenges that shake us to the core.

- A sudden loss
- A medical emergency
- An unexpected financial crisis

Without preparation, these moments can spiral from painful to
chaotic.

This book is your roadmap to proactive protection—a simple,
powerful approach to getting your affairs in order before life
demands it.

You don't need to be an expert in HR, finance, or law. You only
need the willingness to take small, steady steps that shield you and
your loved ones from future stress and confusion.

The Importance of Proactive Preparedness

Many people delay preparation because they believe:
- "I'll get to it later."
- "I don't know where to start."
- "It's uncomfortable to talk about these things."
- "Nothing bad will happen anytime soon."

But life doesn't wait until you feel ready.
Emergencies arrive without warning.

One moment can have your family scrambling for documents, decisions, and resources they aren't prepared to handle.

Proactive preparedness isn't about fear.
It's about love, protection, and responsibility.

It's about making sure your loved ones are not burdened by unanswered questions or financial hardship when life shifts unexpectedly.

How This Book Will Empower You to Take Action

This is not just another book of vague advice.
It's a hands-on blueprint: clear, compassionate, and ready for real life.

Most people don't realize what they need to know until they're already in crisis. But experiencing an emergency is the worst time to start preparing.

This book raises your awareness about the essential documents and plans that become critical when life changes unexpectedly.

It's always better to be ready than to be caught off guard.

In the following chapters, you'll gain:

- **Clear, Step-by-Step Instructions:**
Simple, real-world guidance—no confusing legal jargon.

- **Checklists, Templates, and Tools:**
User-friendly resources to help you organize documents, update beneficiaries, and build your emergency toolkit.

- **Insights into Common Challenges:**
Lessons from real-life experiences to help you avoid preventable mistakes.

- **Tailored Guidance for Different Life Situations:**
Whether you're an employee, entrepreneur, caregiver, or community leader, you'll find advice that fits your journey.

- **Peace of Mind and Empowerment:**
By taking action today, you create stability, clarity, and dignity for yourself and those who depend on you.

The best time to start is now.
Your future self and your loved ones will thank you.

Your journey toward preparedness, protection, and peace of mind begins here.

CHAPTER 1

Facing the Hidden Risks of Being Unprepared

Life can change in an instant: one phone call, one accident, one diagnosis.

Most people think they'll plan later. But the real risk isn't just loss; it's the confusion and hardship that follow when nothing's in place.

Here's what happens without a plan:

- Loved ones are forced to make hard decisions.
- Families end up in court, drained by stress and legal fees.
- Bills, debt, and property become a burden during grief.
- Simple tasks like closing a bank account or selling a car get messy and expensive.

Unpreparedness causes legal delays, emotional strain, broken relationships, and loss of money.

The good news? You don't have to do it all today.
Start small. One step at a time.
This guide will walk you through it, replacing chaos with clarity and stress with peace of mind.

1.1 Common Misconceptions About Emergency Planning

Let's begin by clearing up a few common myths that quietly delay action and leave families unprepared:

Myth 1: "My family knows what I want."
Reality: Verbal conversations are not legally binding, and memories fade under stress.
Consider this: Your loved ones may be left guessing unless your wishes are clearly documented.

Myth 2: "I have life insurance, so I'm covered."
Reality: A policy is only helpful if someone knows where it is and how to claim it.
Consider this: Even with coverage, confusion can delay support when it's needed most.

Myth 3: "I don't have enough assets to need a will."
Reality: A will protects more than just money. It safeguards your belongings, home, and final wishes.
Consider this: Without one, your voice may be lost in decisions about what matters most to you.

Myth 4: "I'll get to it later."
Reality: Emergencies don't wait for the perfect time.
Consider this: What you delay today could become someone else's emergency tomorrow.

Myth 5: "Planning is too complicated."
Reality: Most protective steps are simpler than people think, and help is available.
Consider this: A few basic choices now can save your loved ones months of stress later.

You don't have to figure everything out today, but starting now makes all the difference. In the pages ahead, you'll learn how to take small, manageable steps toward real protection and peace of mind.

1.2 The Real Cost of Delaying Documentation and Decisions

Many people wait too long to prepare because they feel overwhelmed, unsure where to start, or simply assume "it won't happen to me." But delaying doesn't just affect you. It impacts the people who love you, depend on you, and will one day need to make decisions on your behalf.

Here's what can happen when key documents and decisions are missing:

Financial Confusion and Delays

If the person handling finances becomes incapacitated or passes unexpectedly, bills may go unpaid, accounts can freeze, and access to funds may be delayed.

Legal Disputes and Family Conflict

Without a will or updated beneficiaries, even close families can experience tension, court battles, or fractured relationships over who gets what.

> More than **$10 billion** in life insurance benefits in the U.S. have gone unclaimed simply because families didn't know the policies existed (NAIC, 2023).
> That's generational wealth lost. Stability delayed. Peace postponed.
> Most of it could've been preserved with one clear conversation and a documented plan.
> Proactive communication doesn't just protect money—it protects your legacy and the hearts of those you love.

Misguided Medical Decisions

Without clear healthcare instructions, medical teams may rely on the default next of kin, even if that person isn't aligned with your wishes or values.

Emotional and Financial Fallout

The ripple effects of being unprepared can include:

- Heightened stress
- Unresolved grief
- Lingering confusion
- Financial loss

When you're unprepared, the burden falls on the very people you love most, often during a time of crisis. But when you plan ahead, you leave a lasting gift: **clarity, confidence, and peace**.

1.3 What You'll Learn in This Book

In the chapters ahead, you'll learn how to:

- Identify the most important documents for your life.
- Understand their purpose and power.
- Begin taking simple, meaningful steps toward lifelong protection.

You're not just preparing paperwork.
You're preparing a plan that speaks for you, honors your values, and protects your peace, no matter what comes your way.

PART 1

Be Proactive, Not Reactive—Laying a Solid Foundation

You don't have to wait for an emergency to take action.
You can choose clarity, calm, and confidence—right now.

The chapters ahead are designed to help you build a stronger foundation for a life that feels more secure, organized, and empowered, no matter what comes your way. You'll begin gathering key documents, making thoughtful choices, and creating a structure that brings peace of mind, not just for you, but for those who may one day need to support you.

This isn't about fear.
It's about wisdom, dignity, and being one step ahead, because you and your future are worth preparing for.

The following four chapters are a loving first step. Take your time, and move at your own pace. Progress is what matters—and you're already on the right path.

Let's begin together.

CHAPTER 2

Your Essential Documents Checklist

Protecting Your Future with Preparation

Now that you understand the hidden risks of being unprepared, it's time to take the first empowered step toward protecting your future. This chapter is where *awareness* becomes *action*.

You're about to learn what essential documents you need, why each one matters, and how they work together to create a safety net for you and your loved ones. Whether you're just starting or updating what you already have, this checklist will guide you with clarity, care, and confidence.

Keep in mind that not every document will apply to your current situation. Focus only on what's relevant right now. If you realize something is missing, don't panic. Simply make a note to request a replacement and update your records once it arrives.
This process is not about perfection; it's about progress.

For a complete summary, see the ***Master Checklist: Essential Documents Overview*** in Appendix C.

Progress is powerful.
Each document you secure is an act of protection, preparation, and peace of mind.

Let's begin building the foundation that supports every other step in your journey to preparedness.

2.1 Identity & Personal Records

These documents form the backbone of your legal, financial, and healthcare rights.

Without them, accessing services, verifying identity, or advocating for yourself or your dependents can be difficult or even impossible.

Checklist Items (for you, your spouse, and dependents):

- Birth Certificates: Needed for Social Security, passports, insurance, and more.

- Social Security Cards: Required for employment, taxes, benefits, and financial accounts.

- Government-Issued IDs (passport, driver's license, state ID): Used for travel, voting, legal, and financial purposes.

- Citizenship or Immigration Papers: Proves legal status for work, travel, and services.

- Name Change Documents (if applicable): Updates records after marriage, divorce, or personal change.

Secure your primary identity documents now, before a crisis arises. Having them accessible protects your ability to act quickly and receive vital services.

2.2 Marital & Family Documents

These documents legally establish and protect family relationships. They are essential when making decisions about health, finances, custody, and inheritance.

Checklist Items:

- Marriage Certificate: Proof for benefits, insurance, taxes, and next-of-kin rights.

- Divorce Decree/Separation Agreement: Updates legal, financial, and insurance records.

- Prenuptial/Postnuptial Agreement: Defines financial terms during or after marriage.

- Adoption Records: Needed for benefits, tax filings, and school enrollment.

- Custody Agreements and Child Support Orders: Clarifies legal and support arrangements.

- Legal Guardianship Documents: Authorizes decisions for minors or dependents with special needs.

Update these documents as life changes. Keeping them current prevents delays and ensures your wishes are honored.

2.3 Property & Real Estate Documents

Property records confirm ownership and clarify responsibilities. Whether you rent or own, these documents protect your assets, support insurance claims, and make transitions smoother.

Checklist Items:

- Property Deeds and Titles: Proof of ownership for homes, land, and vehicles.

- Mortgage and Loan Agreements: Details financing terms.

- Lease or Rental Agreements: Verifies residence and tenant rights.

- Property Tax Records: Tracks payments and property values.

- Homeowners or Renters Insurance Policies: Essential for property loss or liability coverage.

Organized property documents allow you to act quickly and confidently in the event of loss, sale, dispute, or disaster.

2.4 Financial Records

Financial records offer a clear view of your income, debts, and assets. Organized financial documents support sound decision-making and reduce stress during emergencies.

Checklist Items:

- Tax Returns (last 3–5 years): Used for audits, loans, and legal matters.

- Bank Statements: Tracks account activity and balances.

- Investment and Retirement Statements: Monitors assets for planning and estate purposes.

- Credit Card Statements: Helps manage and resolve debts.

- Loan Agreements: Tracks obligations and repayment terms.

- Pay Stubs or Profit-and-Loss Statements: Verifies income for benefits or loans.

Organized finances reduce stress and support your ability, or someone else's, to manage your affairs with confidence and clarity.

2.5 Insurance Policies

Insurance offers peace of mind—*but only if it's accessible when needed.* Be sure trusted contacts know where to find your policies so they can act without delay.

Checklist Items:

- Life Insurance: Financial support for loved ones after your passing.

- Health Insurance: Proof of medical coverage and benefits.

- Disability Insurance: Income replacement if you can't work.

- Long-Term Care Insurance: Covers ongoing care services.

- Auto Insurance: Required for legal driving and claims.

- Homeowners or Renters Insurance: Protects your property.

- Umbrella Policy: Additional coverage beyond standard policies.

An insurance policy that no one can locate is no protection at all. Make sure they're visible, current, and shared with at least one person you trust.

2.6 Estate Planning Documents

These documents ensure your wishes are honored and your loved ones are cared for, both during incapacity and after death. Proactive planning avoids confusion, court battles, and unnecessary stress.

Checklist Items:

- Last Will and Testament: Directs assets and guardianship decisions.

- Codicils: Updates or revises an existing will.

- Trust Documents: Manages assets and avoids probate.

- Financial Power of Attorney: Designates someone to manage finances.

- Medical Power of Attorney: Authorizes healthcare decisions.

- Living Will/Advance Directive: States treatment preferences.

- Beneficiary Designation Forms: Directly names beneficiaries.

- Letter of Instruction: Offers non-legal guidance for family members.

Estate planning is an act of love. These documents speak for you when you can't—and protect your legacy with honor and clarity.

2.7 Business Documents (If Applicable)

If you own a business, whether full-time, part-time, or as a side venture, your records are part of your personal legacy. Organized business documents protect your hard work, clarify operations, and ensure continuity when it matters most. Your business deserves the same care and protection as any other valuable asset in your life.

Checklist Items:

- Formation Documents: Proves business structure.
- Licenses and Permits: Required for legal operation.
- Operating Agreements: Outlines roles and responsibilities.
- Business Insurance Policies: Shields from liability and disruption.
- Succession Plan: Ensures leadership and ownership transition.

Treat your business like a critical asset—it deserves protection.

2.8 Additional Important Records

These often-overlooked documents support daily life and fill the gaps that broader planning may miss. They add an extra layer of protection and ensure no critical detail is left behind.

Checklist Items:

- Educational Records: Verifies credentials and degrees.
- Medical and Immunization Records: Required for school, travel, and care.
- Vehicle Titles and Registrations: Needed for ownership and resale.

- Major Purchase Receipts: Proves ownership for claims and resale.

- Charitable Contribution Records: Supports tax deductions and estate wishes.

- Safe Deposit Box Inventory: Tracks valuables.

- Digital Asset Information: Logins and access for online accounts.

Once you've gathered your documents, don't stop there. Now is the perfect time to give each one a quick review to ensure it's accurate, signed, and still reflects your current wishes. The next section will show you how.

2.9 How to Review and Audit Documents for Accuracy

Gathering your documents is a powerful first step.
Just as important is making sure they're correct, current, and complete.

Even small mistakes—like a wrong address, an outdated beneficiary, or a missing signature—can lead to major delays, lost money, or legal problems during a crisis. A quick review now can save your loved ones from stress and confusion later.

Why Regular Reviews Matter

Life changes.
Marriages, births, moves, deaths—even changes in the law—can make your documents outdated without you realizing it.

That's why regular reviews are key.
They help keep your paperwork active, accurate, and in line with your current wishes.

Common Mistakes to Look For

- **Incorrect or Outdated Names**
  Misspelled names, outdated beneficiaries, or people who have passed away are still listed.

- **Wrong or Old Addresses**
  Mailing addresses or property details that are no longer accurate.

- **Missing Signatures or Notary Stamps**
  Unsigned documents or those that are missing required legal seals.

- **Outdated Beneficiary Choices**
  Beneficiaries are not updated after a major life event like marriage, divorce, or the loss of a loved one.

Beneficiary Forms Override Wills.

If your will says one thing, but your beneficiary form says another, the beneficiary form wins.*

This applies to life insurance, retirement accounts, and other financial assets.

Always review your beneficiary forms after:

- Marriage or divorce
- Birth or adoption of a child
- The death of a loved one
- Any major change in your life or relationships

Make sure the names listed still reflect your wishes, and that the beneficiary forms are signed and valid.

(*Source: The U.S. Securities and Exchange Commission and the American Bar Association both confirm that beneficiary forms take legal precedence over wills when it comes to financial accounts.)

Bonus Wisdom! Make Sure Someone Knows:

It's not enough to update your documents. Trusted individuals must know they exist and where to find them.

Options include:

- Sharing key information with your executor, power of attorney, or a trusted family member.
- Creating a secure digital vault or sealed envelope listing your critical accounts and policies.
- Including clear written instructions in your estate planning documents.

The goal: Make it easy for your wishes to be honored without a scavenger hunt during a time of grief.

2.10 Managing Your Digital Assets: Passwords, Devices, and Online Accounts

In today's world, being prepared means more than gathering physical paperwork.

It also means protecting your **digital life**: your passwords, devices, and online accounts.

Many of your most important assets and memories now live online. Without a plan, they can be lost, locked away, or left vulnerable.

Taking care of your digital world is just as important as organizing your physical one. It helps protect your identity, your finances, and your legacy.

Why Digital Asset Management Matters

Think of how much of your life is online today:

- Bank and investment accounts
- Health portals with your medical records
- Email and messaging apps
- Family photos, videos, and social media accounts
- Business tools and websites
- Subscriptions and memberships that auto-renew

If no one can access these when needed, it can lead to confusion, stress, and even financial loss.

What to Include in Your Digital Asset Inventory

- **Financial Accounts**
Bank logins, investment platforms, crypto wallets, payment apps (like PayPal, Cash App, or Venmo).

- **Communication and Media**
Email accounts, social media profiles, and cloud storage (Google Drive, iCloud, Dropbox).

- **Business and Professional Accounts**
Websites, domain names, e-commerce stores, and freelance platforms.

- **Devices and Hardware**
Passwords or PINs for your phone, laptop, tablet, or external drives.

- **Subscription Services**
Streaming services, software tools, monthly memberships, and delivery apps.

Best Practices for Digital Organization

- **Use a Password Manager**

Securely store all your logins in apps like LastPass, 1Password, or Bitwarden.

- **Create a Digital Inventory**

Make a list of your key accounts, devices, and subscriptions. Note where the passwords are stored safely.

- **Choose a Digital Trustee**

Select someone you trust to manage your digital life if needed. You may also want to set up a digital power of attorney.

- **Update Backup Info**

Make sure your recovery emails, security questions, and phone numbers are up to date.

- **Tell Someone You Trust**

Let a trusted person know where your digital inventory is stored and how to access it when needed.

Bonus Tips for Safe Digital Legacy Planning

- **Assign a Legacy Contact**

Some platforms (like Facebook and Instagram) let you assign someone to manage your account after you pass away.

- **Write a Digital Goodbye Letter**

Leave final instructions or personal messages. Store them securely alongside your digital inventory.

- **List Your Subscriptions**

Make it easy for someone to cancel auto-renewals and avoid unwanted charges.

- **Back Up Digital Memories**
Save photos, videos, and important messages to a cloud drive or external hard drive for safekeeping.

To make this step easier, you'll find a *Quick Digital Inventory Template* in Appendix D. It's a sample layout showing how to organize your key accounts, devices, and digital tools in one place.

Use it as a guide to create your own version, and store a printed copy with your emergency binder. Review and update it once a year to keep your digital life current and protected.

CHAPTER 3

Building Your Emergency Toolkit

Creating Quick-Access Tools for Life's Critical Moments

With your essential documents gathered and understood, you've built a strong foundation. Now, it's time to turn that preparation into *actionable protection*. This chapter is about making your information *usable* in real life, during moments when clarity, speed, and access can save lives.

You'll now learn how to create simple yet powerful tools that help you, your loved ones, and first responders make quick, informed decisions in a crisis. From medical emergencies to natural disasters, your emergency toolkit will ensure that vital information is always within reach—organized, accessible, and ready when it's needed most.

Why We Start with Medical Emergencies

In any serious emergency, saving a life comes first.
Financial and legal matters can wait, but doctors and first responders need accurate information *immediately* to provide the right care.

That's why we begin this chapter by focusing on your **Hospital Emergency Plan Essentials**—the most critical details that must be ready at a moment's notice.

Once that plan is in place, we'll expand to create broader emergency toolkits that protect every other part of your life: before, during, and after a crisis.

What You'll Build in This Chapter

By the end of this chapter, you will have created four simple yet powerful tools that can support you and your loved ones during an emergency:

- A **Hospital Emergency Plan** to guide urgent medical care.
- An **ICE (In Case of Emergency) Plan** to support a quick family response.
- An **Emergency Preparedness Binder** to keep your key documents organized and ready.
- A **Document Location Summary**: a one-page guide showing exactly where your essential records are stored.

Together, these tools form the heart of your emergency response system. Whether you're facing a health crisis, a natural disaster, or simply preparing for peace of mind, they give you and your family the confidence to act quickly, clearly, and with care.

This is more than just organization.
It's a quiet act of leadership and love that honors your future and protects those who may one day have to step in on your behalf.

How This Chapter Is Organized

We'll walk through each toolkit using:

- Clear, actionable checklists
- Simple, real-life examples
- Practical tips for keeping everything updated and accessible

You don't need special skills, legal training, or expensive tools to get started. All you need is a willingness to prepare and the belief that your life and the lives of those you love are worth protecting.

3.1 Hospital Emergency Plan Essentials

What an Emergency Room Physician Wants You to Know

In a critical emergency, every second matters. Having the right information on hand can mean the difference between delay and decisive action. Below is expert input from an emergency room physician on what helps the medical team respond swiftly, safely, and in alignment with your wishes.

Critical Information for Your Hospital Emergency Plan:

- **Blood Type & Rh Factor**
Knowing this allows for immediate blood transfusions. Without it, the hospital must run tests, which takes time that may not be available.

- **Medication List**
This is one of the most critical pieces of information. It helps avoid dangerous drug interactions and informs care, especially for patients on insulin, heart medications, blood thinners, or psychiatric prescriptions.

- **Medical Conditions & Surgical History**
Diagnoses like diabetes, epilepsy, or heart disease guide treatment decisions. Past surgeries and any implanted devices (like pacemakers or joint replacements) also impact care.

- **Health Insurance Information**
It is not essential in the first few minutes of care, but it is important for hospital admission, care coordination, and follow-up. Having this ready reduces delays and billing complications.

- **Advance Directive or Medical Power of Attorney**
We need to know who is legally authorized to speak on behalf of the patient. If this isn't documented, we may have to

act without clear consent, even against the patient's known preferences.

- **Emergency Contacts**

This information is vital for both emotional support and critical decision-making. Make sure it's clear who is authorized to receive updates and make healthcare choices.

- **Photo ID**

Add a copy of a driver's license, state ID, or passport. This helps verify the patient's identity, especially if they're unconscious, non-verbal, or brought in without personal items.

- **DNR Order (if applicable)**

If a "Do Not Resuscitate" order exists, it must be available in writing. Without it, we are legally obligated to perform full life-saving measures.

Additional Information That Makes a Difference

- **Primary Care Physician or Specialist Contact Information**

If we need more context or medical history, this allows us to reach the doctors who know the patient best.

- **Known Language Barriers or Disabilities**

If the patient is deaf, hard of hearing, non-verbal, visually impaired, or does not speak English, we can better accommodate them if we're informed up front.

Final Thoughts from the Physician

"When families walk into the ER with this kind of preparation, it changes everything. We move faster. We make safer decisions. We feel confident in honoring the patient's wishes. Most importantly, we can focus on saving the person in front of us, not scrambling for answers."

Pro Tip: Keep It Ready and Clearly Labeled

Store each person's Hospital Emergency Plan in a clearly labeled physical or digital folder for fast access during a crisis.

Example Labels:

- Hospital Plan – Meredith Grey
- Hospital Plan – Derek Shepherd

Use color-coded folders if helpful, and keep them in a central location such as:

- An emergency go bag
- A home safe
- A secure digital file labeled "Medical Emergency Plans"

These small steps today become *protection* tomorrow for you and the ones who love you.

3.2 What Is an ICE (In Case of Emergency) Plan?

Protecting Your Voice When You Can't Speak for Yourself

In an emergency, decisions still need to be made, even if you're unable to make them yourself. An ICE (In Case of Emergency) Plan equips your trusted inner circle with the essential information they need to act on your behalf without confusion or delay.

While a Hospital Emergency Plan protects *your life*, an ICE Plan protects *your responsibilities, your dependents, and your voice*.

Purpose of an ICE Plan

An ICE Plan empowers your loved ones to:

- Make urgent medical, financial, or legal decisions in alignment with your wishes.

- Protect your family, dependents, pets, and property.
- Handle time-sensitive matters without roadblocks or guesswork.

It's not just personal protection—it's a proactive system of care for everything and everyone that depends on you.

Who Should Have Access to Your ICE Plan

Only share your ICE Plan with individuals who hold legal authority or critical roles in your emergency response network. This may include:

- Your power of attorney
- Your medical proxy
- Your executor
- Key family members or professional advisors

Clear roles and mutual trust are essential. Keep access limited to those who *need to know* in order to act responsibly on your behalf.

Essential Items to Include in Your ICE Plan

A complete ICE Plan covers three key areas:

1. Emergency Contacts

- Primary and backup contacts (full names, relationships, phone numbers, and emails)
- Medical power of attorney or healthcare proxy
- Financial power of attorney or estate executor

2. Medical Information

- Location of your Hospital Emergency Plan
- Copies or summaries of your advance healthcare directives

- Basic insurance details for quick decision-making

3. Immediate Action Instructions

- Who should be contacted right away (family, employer, attorney, etc.)
- Instructions for dependents (e.g., pick-up procedures, temporary guardianship)
- Instructions for pets (e.g., feeding, emergency care, vet contacts)
- Property management tasks (e.g., securing the home, paying urgent bills, turning off utilities, accessing keys or alarm codes)
- Secure access to key digital accounts or a password manager, if needed

Best Practices for Storing and Sharing Your ICE Plan

Physical Copy:

Keep a printed copy in a fireproof safe or other secure, accessible location.

Digital Copy:

Store an encrypted version in secure cloud storage.

Be sure to share access instructions with your power of attorney, medical proxy, and executor.

Access Instructions:

Make sure your trusted individuals know:

- Where your ICE Plan is stored
- How to use it

- When to activate it

Your ICE Plan is your voice when you cannot speak, your hands when you cannot act, and your love in motion when you cannot be present.

Prepare it now, so that your values, your responsibilities, and the people who depend on you are protected when it matters most.

3.3 Creating Your Emergency Preparedness Binder

Your Personal Command Center in a Crisis

In Chapter 2, we gathered your essential documents. Now, we'll take the next step: organizing them into your Emergency Preparedness Binder.

When emergencies strike, having everything in one place can turn chaos into calm. An Emergency Preparedness Binder is a simple, structured collection of your most important personal, legal, medical, and financial documents—ready when you or your loved ones need them most.

Unlike the Hospital Emergency Plan, which focuses on life-saving medical care, this binder safeguards your finances, property, identity, and final wishes. It becomes a trusted guide for your family, attorney, or executor if you're ever hospitalized, incapacitated, or pass away unexpectedly.

Start Where You Are: Progress Over Perfection

You don't need fancy supplies to begin.
A basic binder from a dollar store is enough to start protecting yourself and your family.

Gather what you have now. Upgrade later if needed.
Don't wait for the perfect moment—*start now, protect now,* and

build as you go.

What Makes a Strong Binder System

Your binder should be:

- **Simple** – Easy to understand at a glance
- **Organized** – Clearly divided into labeled sections
- **Secure** – Stored safely but easy to access when needed
- **Updated** – Reviewed at least once a year or after major life changes

Think of this binder as your life's **command center**—a tool that gives clarity and confidence to those who may need to act on your behalf.

Key Sections to Include

1. Personal Information

- Full name, date of birth, and Social Security number
- Copies of IDs: driver's license, passport, etc.
- Birth certificate, marriage/divorce documents, custody papers
- Military discharge paperwork (if applicable)

2. Financial Information

- Bank and credit account details
- Investment and retirement accounts (401(k), IRAs, etc.)
- Mortgage and loan documents
- Records of income sources (job, pension, rental, etc.)

3. Legal Documents

- Last will and testament
- Living trust (if applicable)
- Powers of attorney (medical and financial)
- Advance healthcare directive/living will
- HIPAA authorization forms

4. Property & Asset Information

- Property deeds or lease, insurance policies, HOA docs
- Utility account information (electric, gas, water, internet)
- Vehicle titles and registration
- List of high-value personal property
- Spare keys and home security codes

5. Funeral & Final Wishes

- Burial or cremation preferences
- Funeral home details or instructions
- Obituary preferences
- Optional: Personal letters to loved ones

6. Digital Assets & Online Accounts

- Password manager details and master login location
- List of key financial, email, and social media accounts
- Access instructions for phones, tablets, laptops, and cloud storage
- Digital subscription and auto-renewal service list
- Assigned legacy contacts for online platforms

- Optional: Personal instructions or digital goodbye letter

Affordable Supplies to Get Started

Essentials:

- Three-ring binder
- Tab dividers
- Sheet protectors
- Optional: zippered pouch for keys or USB drives

Upgrades (if desired):

- Fireproof, waterproof document safe
- Pre-labeled document organizers

Where to Store Your Binder

- Keep a physical copy in a fireproof, accessible place.
- Store a digital backup in encrypted cloud storage or a password-protected USB.
- Make sure your power of attorney, medical proxy, and executor know how to access it.

Choosing Who Gets Access

Select someone who is calm, dependable, and honors your values. Walk them through the binder while you're well, and make sure they understand your intentions. Provide both printed and digital access, along with passwords, if necessary.

Final Note: Why This Matters

This isn't about fear; it's about *love, leadership, and legacy.*
By creating this binder, you offer a lifeline of clarity for the people who love you most. You're building a protective system that speaks

when you can't and safeguards your family's future.

You don't have to do it all at once.
Start with one section, one document, one step. That single act of preparation can change everything.

Tip:

Keep your Emergency Preparedness Binder packed with your "go bag" for fast evacuation, just in case.

Now that you've created your Hospital Emergency Plan, assembled your ICE (In Case of Emergency) Plan, and built your Emergency Preparedness Binder, there's just one final step to tie it all together. Create a simple one-page summary that tells your trusted people *where everything lives*.

This tool may seem small, but it can make all the difference in an urgent situation, especially when time, clarity, and direction matter most.

3.4 Document Location Summary

Quick Access Guide for Trusted Contacts

This one-page summary helps your trusted individuals know *where your Emergency Preparedness Binder is stored* and how your essential documents are organized. It's not a list of every document—just a high-level roadmap showing what category holds what type of information and where everything is located.

Keep this summary at the very front of your binder and share a copy with your medical proxy, power of attorney, or executor as needed.

Where My Emergency Documents Are Stored:

- Physical Binder Location: [Insert location, e.g., "Top shelf of home office fireproof safe"]

- Digital Backup Location: [Insert, e.g., "Encrypted cloud folder – link shared with POA and Executor"]

What's Inside My Emergency Preparedness Binder (by Section):

1. **Hospital Emergency Plan**
   Includes: Medical summary, medication list, insurance cards, medical power of attorney, DNR (if applicable)

2. **ICE (In Case of Emergency) Plan**
   Includes: Emergency contacts, instructions for children or dependents, pet care plan, digital account access, and household management instructions

3. **Personal Information**
   Includes: Birth certificate, Social Security number, ID copies, marriage/divorce records, military discharge papers

4. **Financial Information**
   Includes: Bank accounts, credit card summaries, investment and retirement account statements, loan documents, income sources

5. **Legal Documents**
   Includes: Will, living trust, powers of attorney, advance healthcare directive, HIPAA forms

6. **Property & Assets**
   Includes: Property deeds or lease agreements, utility accounts, home security codes, vehicle titles, personal property inventory, spare keys

7. **Funeral & Final Wishes**
   Includes: Burial or cremation preferences, funeral home details, obituary notes, personal letters (optional)

8. **Digital Assets & Online Accounts**
   Includes: Digital inventory template, password manager info, device access instructions, list of subscriptions, legacy contact notes

Spotlight: Life Insurance Policy – Critical Document

My life insurance policy is stored in: [Insert location, e.g., "Binder – Section 4: Property & Assets"]

Why This Matters:

In many emergencies, families struggle to locate the life insurance policy, delaying access to vital financial support during the hardest time. This document is essential to settle final expenses, support dependents, and avoid unnecessary financial hardship. Ensure at least one trusted person knows exactly where to find it.

Trusted Individuals with Access:

- Medical Proxy: [Insert name]
- Power of Attorney: [Insert name]
- Executor: [Insert name]
- Additional Contact (if any): [Insert name]

Review Reminder:

Update this summary whenever you change the storage location of your documents, update access permissions, or make changes to your binder contents.

CHAPTER 4

Communicating with Loved Ones

Now that you've begun organizing your documents, creating emergency kits, and thinking ahead with intention, it's time to take the next powerful step: sharing that wisdom with the people who matter most.

Communication is the heartbeat of preparation.

Even the most well-prepared plan can fall short if no one knows it exists. Communication is what transforms your private preparations into collective protection.

Everyone's family dynamic is different. Some readers may feel fully supported, while others carry the weight of responsibility alone. Regardless of your situation, this chapter is here to help you communicate from a place of peace, not pressure, meeting your loved ones wherever they are on their own journey.

You're about to learn how to begin these conversations with calmness, courage, and compassion. Whether you're sharing your plan, checking in with loved ones, or gently planting the seed of preparedness, this is where quiet action becomes shared peace of mind.

For extra support, you'll find a list of gentle conversation starters in Appendix E, titled *Conversation Starters: Communicating with Loved Ones*. These questions are grouped by topic—like hospital planning, adult children, or aging parents—to help you approach each discussion with clarity, compassion, and care.

4.1 Preparing for Conversations About Emergency Planning

Talking about emergencies can feel awkward, but starting the conversation is one of the most loving and protective things you can do.

When you lead with composure, insight, and care, you make it easier for everyone involved. You're not being negative; you're being proactive.

How to Prepare Yourself

- **Get clear on what you want to share.**

  Example: "I put together a binder with my emergency contacts, health info, and ID. I just want you to know where it is."

- **Be honest about the decisions you've made.**

  Example: "I chose my best friend as my medical proxy since she lives close by and knows my wishes."

- **Think of a few gentle questions to ask.**

  Example: "Have you written down your emergency contacts or healthcare wishes yet?"

- **Know your goal.**

  Are you planting a seed? Sharing your plan? Offering help?

  Example: "I just want you to know I've made a plan. We can talk about yours whenever you feel ready."

- **Consider a written follow-up.**

  After your conversation, consider sharing a brief summary, like where your Emergency Binder is stored or who to contact first. Clear, written notes can offer guidance when emotions are high in a crisis.

Maria S. Turner

Choosing the Right Time and Setting

Pick a moment when everyone is calm, present, and not distracted. A relaxed setting helps make the conversation feel safe.

You might begin with:
"Can we talk for a few minutes? I've been learning how to be better prepared for emergencies and wanted to check in with you about a few things."

Leading the Conversation

Speak with honesty and warmth. Reassure your loved ones that:

- You're not trying to control anyone.
- You're speaking from love, not fear.
- You want to reduce stress and confusion later, not cause worry now.

You might say:
"I'm not expecting anything bad to happen. I just want to make sure we're not left scrambling if something ever comes up."

4.2 Meeting People Where They Are

These conversations won't look the same for everyone. Your loved ones may include a spouse, child, sibling, neighbor, or trusted friend. Some may be open and receptive, while others may feel overwhelmed or avoidant. That's okay.

Stay soft, not forceful. You're planting seeds, not pushing an agenda.

You can gently say:
"I know it's not easy to talk about, but I want us all to be protected. I'm here if you ever want help making your own plan."

Keeping the Door Open

Let them know this doesn't have to be a one-time conversation. Invite them to talk again, whenever they're ready.

- You can share what worked for you.
- You can listen without judgment.
- You can remind them they're not alone.

Preparedness isn't about fear. It's about peace of mind—for them, for you, and for everyone you love.

4.3 Quick Checklist: Before You Start the Conversation

- ✓ I know what I want to share (plans, documents, decisions).
- ✓ I've prepared three gentle questions (on topics such as hospital plan, ICE plan, or binder location).
- ✓ I've chosen a quiet, focused time and place.
- ✓ I've written a few notes to stay calm and clear.
- ✓ I'm ready to listen without judgment and offer support without pressure.

Sharing your plan is one of the greatest gifts you can offer, because clarity today becomes confidence tomorrow.

PART 2

Prepared, Not Panicked—Navigating Life's Unexpected Moments

In the remaining chapters, I'm sharing what 17 years of working in Human Resources taught me—not just from policies and procedures, but from real stories and tender conversations. I've listened to colleagues, friends, and family go through emergencies they never expected. And what I've discovered is this: you don't have to wait for a challenge to learn the hard way. You can prepare from wisdom, not just experience.

Most people, if not everyone, will face at least one of the scenarios in these chapters during their lifetime. Many will face multiple.

This guide is here to help you move through real-life situations with clarity, confidence, and calmness. It offers high-level action steps you can take when time is short, emotions are high, and decisions still need to be made.

And for those moments when you need extra support? Be sure to explore ***Appendix F: Helpful Programs to Know About*** at the end of this book. It includes a curated list of real-world resources from meal delivery to burial assistance, financial aid, caregiver tools, legal help, and more. These aren't just links; they're starting points. While not every program will apply to every reader, each one is worth knowing about.

If you are currently employed, one of the most underutilized—but highly valuable—resources may already be available: your **Employee Assistance Program (EAP)**. These programs are often provided by employers at no cost and can offer confidential support with grief, legal advice, financial stress, caregiving needs, and mental health services. Don't wait until you're overwhelmed to ask what's available. Reach out to your HR department to learn more. You may be more supported than you think.

Because when you know better, you're equipped to help someone else do the same.

Each one reach one.
Each one teach one.

CHAPTER 5

Health and Caregiving Challenges

Health emergencies can change life overnight.
This chapter gives clear guidance for managing serious illnesses, supporting loved ones through crises, and handling long-term caregiving with steadiness and care. Whether the challenge is physical, mental, or emotional, you'll find guidance to stay grounded and make strong decisions during vulnerable times. A little preparation now offers peace of mind later.

During a health crisis, it's important to remember that you're not alone. Within hospital settings, professionals such as **patient advocates, social workers,** and **case managers** are available to help you or your loved one navigate the next steps. They can clarify the care process, connect you to resources, and prepare you for life after discharge. *If you ever feel overwhelmed, confused, or unsupported—do not hesitate to ask to speak with one of these professionals.* They are there to walk beside you with compassion and provide clarity.

Topics Covered:

- Managing a Serious Health Condition
- Supporting a Loved One Facing a Health Crisis
- Navigating an Unexpected Hospitalization
- Coping with a Mental Health Crisis
- Living with Chronic Illness or Long-Term Disability
- Becoming a Family Caregiver
- Caring for a Child with Special Needs into Adulthood

5.1 Managing a Serious Health Condition

A sudden illness or chronic condition can disrupt your ability to work, manage finances, and make decisions. Without a plan, you risk income loss, rising medical bills, and barriers to getting the care you want.

How to Prepare:

- **Create an Advance Healthcare Directive and Medical Power of Attorney (POA):**
  Spell out your medical wishes and name someone you trust to make decisions if you can't.

- **Secure Disability or Income Protection:**
  If *employed*: Review your employer's short-term disability benefits.
  If *self-employed*: Look into private disability insurance or build emergency savings.
  If *retired or unemployed*: Explore long-term care insurance, Medicaid, SSDI, or VA benefits if eligible.

- **Grant Access to Key Information:**
  Store insurance documents, medical history, and emergency contacts in a secure place. Give a trusted person legal access to manage affairs if needed.

- **Plan for Household and Financial Management:**
  Set up automatic payments for essential bills.
  Consider assigning a financial POA to manage accounts during incapacity.

- **Plan for Temporary Guardianship (if applicable):**
  If you are the parent or legal guardian of a minor child, consider putting a temporary guardianship plan in place in case a health emergency prevents you from caring for them.

Maria S. Turner

Naming a trusted temporary caregiver ahead of time—
ideally in a notarized document—can help avoid last-minute
decisions, court delays, or unexpected involvement from
child protective services.

Immediate Steps in a Health Crisis:

- Make sure your healthcare proxy and family have copies
of your directives.
- Notify your employer or disability insurer to activate
benefits.
- Assign someone to manage finances and prevent missed
payments.
- Confirm insurance coverage and expected costs if
hospitalized.
- If you become unable to care for your child or children,
activate your temporary guardianship plan or contact a
trusted adult immediately to step in while legal steps are
taken.

Helpful Resources:

- Healthcare.gov – Health insurance and patient rights
- DOL.gov/FMLA – Family and Medical Leave Act
protections
- SSA.gov – Social Security Disability benefits
- PatientAdvocate.org – Help with medical bill negotiations
- MentalHealth.gov – Mental health support and resources

5.2 Supporting a Loved One Facing a Health Crisis

Caring for a sick or injured loved one can strain your finances, job security, and emotional health. Without preparation, caregiving can quickly lead to financial instability and burnout.

How to Prepare:

- **Understand the Family and Medical Leave Act (FMLA) and Paid Leave Options:**
  Check if you qualify for job-protected leave under the Family and Medical Leave Act (FMLA).
  Explore state-paid family leave and employer caregiver benefits.

- **Set Up Medical and Legal Protections:**
  Make sure your loved one has a healthcare directive, medical power of attorney (POA), and a completed HIPAA Authorization Form to allow trusted individuals access to their medical records.
  Review their health insurance and financial resources.

- **Prepare for Potential Income Loss:**
  Assess your savings, disability benefits, and available caregiver grants.

- **Establish a Support Network:**
  Organize help from family, friends, or professional caregivers to avoid burnout.

- **Plan for Temporary Guardianship (if applicable):**
  If your loved one is a parent or legal guardian, encourage them to consider naming a trusted temporary caregiver in case a health emergency or crisis prevents them from caring for their child. Having a simple plan in writing—ideally notarized—can help avoid last-minute decisions, court

delays, or unexpected involvement from child protective services.

Immediate Steps in a Health Crisis:

- Contact your employer's HR department about FMLA or paid leave options.
- Gather and organize your loved one's medical and legal documents.
- Confirm insurance coverage for immediate care needs.
- Arrange caregiving support to share the load.
- If your loved one becomes unable to care for their child or children, they should activate their temporary guardianship plan or contact a trusted adult immediately to step in while legal steps are taken.

Helpful Resources:

- DOL.gov/FMLA – Family and Medical Leave Act (FMLA) information
- Medicaid.gov – Medicaid caregiver benefits and stipends
- SSA.gov – Social Security Disability Insurance (SSDI) resources
- Caregiver.org – Caregiver assistance and grant programs
- MentalHealth.gov – Mental health support for caregivers

5.3 Navigating an Unexpected Hospitalization

A sudden hospitalization can leave financial, legal, and caregiving gaps if no one is prepared to step in. Planning ahead helps protect what matters most, without adding extra stress in a crisis.

How to Prepare:

- **Review Your Hospital Emergency Plan:**
  Make sure your trusted contacts can quickly access your plan, including access to insurance cards, medication lists, and medical documents.
  (See Section 3.1: Hospital Emergency Plan Essentials.)

- **Set Up Financial Protections:**
  Automate bill payments.
  Assign a financial power of attorney to manage accounts if needed.

- **Understand Your Health Insurance:**
  Review your deductible, co-pays, and out-of-pocket max.
  Plan ahead for rehab, transportation, or in-home care after discharge.

- **Plan for Temporary Guardianship (if applicable):**
  If you are the parent or legal guardian of a minor child, consider putting a temporary guardianship plan in place in case a health emergency or crisis prevents you from caring for them. Naming a trusted temporary caregiver ahead of time—ideally in a notarized document—can help avoid last-minute decisions, court delays, or unexpected involvement from child protective services.

Immediate Steps in a Hospitalization Crisis:

- Notify your employer's HR department about leave options under the Family and Medical Leave Act (FMLA), short-term disability, or paid leave.
- Assign someone to handle household, pet, or dependent care.
- Confirm insurance coverage and ask about expected out-of-pocket costs to avoid surprise bills.
- If you become unable to care for your child or children, activate your temporary guardianship plan or contact a trusted adult immediately to step in while legal steps are taken.

Helpful Resources:

- Healthcare.gov – Understanding health insurance
- PatientAdvocate.org – Hospital financial assistance
- Ready.gov – Emergency planning guidance
- FairHealthConsumer.org – Help reviewing medical bills
- Medicare.gov/Discharge-Planning – Patient rights and discharge planning

5.4 Coping with a Mental Health Crisis

Mental health crises can disrupt decision-making, trigger emergency hospitalizations, and lead to job loss and financial instability. Preparation protects your health, rights, and stability when you need it most.

How to Prepare:

- **Create a Mental Health Crisis Plan:**
  Designate a mental health care proxy.
  Research psychiatric advance directives if your state offers them.

- **Understand Workplace Protections:**
  Learn about the Family and Medical Leave Act (FMLA), the Americans with Disabilities Act (ADA), and short-term disability options for mental health leave.

- **Set Up Financial and Legal Safeguards:**
  Assign a financial power of attorney if needed.
  Keep health insurance and mental health documents easily accessible.

- **Plan for Temporary Guardianship (if applicable):**
  If you are the parent or legal guardian of a minor child, consider putting a temporary guardianship plan in place in case a health emergency or crisis prevents you from caring for them. Naming a trusted temporary caregiver ahead of time—ideally in a notarized document—can help avoid last-minute decisions, court delays, or unexpected involvement from child protective services.

Immediate Steps in a Mental Health Crisis:

- Contact a 24/7 crisis helpline or local emergency mental health services.

- Notify your employer's HR department to request leave through FMLA or other programs.

- Confirm insurance coverage for hospitalization, outpatient care, and counseling.

- Connect with trusted family, friends, or professional support networks.

- If you become unable to care for your child or children, activate your temporary guardianship plan or contact a trusted adult immediately to step in while legal steps are taken.

Helpful Resources:

- 988lifeline.org – Suicide and Crisis Lifeline (Call or text 988)

- NAMI.org – National Alliance on Mental Illness – support and education

- ADA.gov – Americans with Disabilities Act (ADA) – employment protections

- DOL.gov/FMLA – Family and Medical Leave Act (FMLA) guidance for mental health leave

- MentalHealth.gov – Financial and legal planning resources

5.5 Living with Chronic Illness or Long-Term Disability

Living with a chronic illness doesn't automatically mean you're legally disabled. Qualification for benefits depends on how much your condition limits your ability to work or manage daily life. If you're unsure, consult your healthcare provider or a disability rights organization. Knowing your options now helps you plan for a stronger future.

A chronic illness or long-term disability can disrupt your career, drain your savings, and threaten your financial stability. Many assume disability benefits will fully protect them, but approvals often take months, and payments rarely replace full income. Without a solid plan, hardship can come fast.

How to Prepare:

- **Understand Your Disability Insurance Options:**
  Employer-provided short-term and long-term disability insurance.
  Private disability insurance (especially for self-employed individuals).
  Social Security Disability Insurance (SSDI) for long-term support.

- **Build an Emergency Financial Plan:**
  Create an emergency fund covering 6–12 months of essential expenses.
  Cut non-essential spending to stretch savings.
  Explore assistance programs like Medicaid, SSDI, and food aid.

- **Plan for Legal and Estate Matters:**
  Assign a financial power of attorney.
  Create a living will to document your healthcare wishes.

Immediate Steps After a Disability Diagnosis:

- File for SSDI and/or private disability benefits immediately (approval can take six months or more).

- Review and update your health insurance for long-term care needs.

- Contact your employer's HR department to discuss leave, accommodations, and benefits.

- Adjust your household budget to reflect reduced or delayed income.

Helpful Resources:

- SSA.gov – Social Security Disability Insurance (SSDI)

- ADA.gov – Disability employment protections

- Medicaid.gov – Long-term care planning

- Benefits.gov – Financial assistance programs

- NFCC.org – Debt and credit counseling services

5.6 Becoming a Family Caregiver

Family caregiving is an act of love, but without preparation, it can bring financial strain, emotional exhaustion, and legal challenges. Caregivers often face lost income, rising expenses, and burnout. Knowing your rights and resources protects both your loved one and your own stability.

How to Prepare:

- **Understand Workplace Rights and Benefits:**
  Review eligibility for Family and Medical Leave Act (FMLA) protections.
  Explore employer-paid family leave or flexible work options.

- **Plan Financially and Legally:**
  Set a caregiving budget.
  Secure power of attorney and healthcare proxy documents.

- **Leverage Government Assistance:**
  Explore Medicaid caregiver compensation programs.
  Apply for Social Security Disability benefits (SSDI or SSI) if your loved one qualifies.

- **Prioritize Emotional Health and Respite Care:**
  Set up respite services, support groups, and caregiver assistance to prevent burnout.

Immediate Steps for New Caregivers:

- Contact your employer's HR department to discuss leave and flexibility.
- Meet with an elder law attorney to secure key legal documents.

- Apply for financial aid programs like Medicaid waivers and disability benefits.
- Build a support network of family, friends, and professional caregivers.
- Schedule regular respite care to protect your emotional and physical health.

Helpful Resources:

- CaregiverAction.org – Family caregiver resources
- ARCH National Respite Network – Respite care programs
- Benefits.gov – Government benefits for caregivers
- DOL.gov/FMLA – Family and Medical Leave Act (FMLA) guidelines
- Medicaid.gov – Medicaid and state caregiver programs

5.7 Caring for a Child with Special Needs into Adulthood

Caring for a child with special needs is a lifelong responsibility that often continues well into adulthood. Without a clear plan, families risk leaving their loved ones financially, medically, and legally vulnerable. Taking action today can secure a stronger, more stable future.

Practical Action Steps:

- **Consult a Special Needs Attorney:**
  Set up legal protections like guardianship, power of attorney, and a Special Needs Trust (SNT) to protect assets and benefits.

- **Apply for Government Benefits Early:**
  Start applications for Supplemental Security Income (SSI), Medicaid, and vocational services before your child turns 18.

- **Create a Long-Term Care Plan:**
  Document housing preferences, daily routines, education goals, and medical needs.

- **Write a Letter of Intent:**
  Leave clear instructions for future caregivers about your child's care, preferences, and values.

- **Connect with Employment Support Services:**
  Explore vocational rehabilitation, supported employment, and Ticket to Work programs.

- **Review and Update Plans Regularly:**
  Adjust documents and strategies as your child's needs evolve.

Common Challenges and Solutions:

- **Loss of Benefits Due to Inheritance:**
  Use a Special Needs Trust to safeguard eligibility.

- **Uncertainty About Future Caregivers:**
  Legally name guardians and successors; update plans as needed.

- **Limited Employment Opportunities:**
  Use job training, supported employment, and disability services.

- **Healthcare Access Challenges:**
  Keep Medicaid enrollment active and explore supplemental insurance options.

Helpful Resources:

- CDC.gov – Disability statistics
- Caregiving.org – Family caregiving support
- AutismSpeaks.org – Lifetime care studies
- SSA.gov – SSI and Ticket to Work programs
- Medicaid.gov – Disability services and benefits
- TheArc.org – Disability advocacy and support
- ABLENRC.org – Financial planning with ABLE accounts
- NDRN.org – Legal assistance for people with disabilities

CHAPTER 6

Family Loss & Grief Events

Guiding Yourself Through Loss with Grace and Strength

Losing a loved one brings emotional and practical challenges. This chapter gives you clear steps for handling urgent legal and personal tasks while creating space to heal. The goal is clarity, dignity, and peace during one of life's hardest seasons.

For extra support, see the ***Soft Timeline for Managing Affairs After a Loss*** and the ***Master List of Places to Notify After a Loved One's Passing*** in the Appendices.

Topics Covered:

- What to Do First After the Loss of a Loved One
- Sudden Loss of a Spouse or Partner
- Loss of a Parent
- Loss of a Minor Child
- Loss of an Adult Child
- Loss of a Sibling or Close Relative

6.1 What to Do First After the Loss of a Loved One

Moving Through the First Steps with Clarity and Care

Grief can make even simple tasks feel overwhelming.
This guide helps you focus on the most urgent actions first, then move through the rest at your own steady pace.

Most Urgent (First 24 – 48 Hours):

- **Secure the Body and Notify Authorities:**
  If death occurs outside a hospital or hospice, call 911.
  If under hospice care, call the hospice agency. A medical professional must officially pronounce the death.

- **Notify Immediate Family or Key Contacts:**
  Tell the closest family members or trusted individuals.
  If needed, delegate sharing the news.

- **Contact a Funeral Home or Cremation Service:**
  Arrange transportation of the body.
  You don't have to plan services yet—focus on respectful care.

- **Secure Their Home and Property:**
  Lock doors and windows.
  Protect valuables, pets, medications, and important documents.

- **Care for Dependents and Pets:**
  Make sure children, elderly parents, or pets have food, shelter, and safety.

Most Important (Within the First Week):

- **Obtain Death Certificates:**
  Order at least 5–10 certified copies through the funeral home or the state's vital records office.

- **Begin Funeral or Memorial Planning:**
  Honor any pre-stated wishes. Choose a service that feels right for your family.

- **Locate Important Documents:**
  Find the will, insurance policies, financial records, military papers, and safe deposit box keys.
  Focus on gathering, not solving.
  (If they created an Emergency Preparedness Binder, see Section 3.3, Step 5: Funeral and Final Wishes.)

- **Notify Employer and Key Institutions:**
  Inform their employer.
  Notify places like banks, insurance companies, and Social Security.
  (See the *Master List of Places to Notify After a Loved One's Passing* in Appendix A.)

- **Honor Your Own Grieving Process:**
  Rest. Hydrate. Accept help.
  You are doing sacred work, tending to a soul's transition and your family's healing.

Soft Reminder:

Urgent steps require attention, but your heart deserves time. Move with care. Ask for help. Offer yourself grace.

6.2 Sudden Loss of a Spouse or Partner

Protecting Yourself Legally and Financially During Grief

Losing a spouse or partner brings deep emotional and financial challenges. Married spouses often have automatic rights; unmarried partners usually do not. Without legal planning, partners may face eviction, asset loss, or financial hardship.

How to Prepare:

- **Update Estate Plans and Beneficiaries:**
  Create a will or trust.
  Name each other as beneficiaries on life insurance, retirement accounts, and financial assets.
  Add both names to property titles when possible.

- **Establish Legal Authority:**
  Set up medical and financial powers of attorney.
  Complete HIPAA forms for medical access.

- **Understand Survivor Benefits:**
  Married spouses may qualify for Social Security, pensions, and life insurance benefits.
  Unmarried partners must be named beneficiaries and may need private legal arrangements.

- **Organize Essential Documents:**
  Secure copies of marriage certificates, wills, insurance policies, and property records.
  Keep them easily accessible for claims and transfers.

Immediate Steps After Losing a Spouse or Partner:

- Obtain multiple certified copies of the death certificate.
- Contact life insurance companies and begin claims.

- Notify Social Security and/or pension administrators for survivor benefits.

- Begin transferring ownership of property titles, financial accounts, and vehicles.

- Review and update your own estate plans and beneficiary designations.

Important Note for Unmarried Partners:
If you're not legally married, the law may not recognize your relationship in critical moments. Without proper legal documents, your partner may be denied inheritance, survivor benefits, shared property rights, or the ability to make medical or financial decisions. To protect each other, ensure your partner is named in writing across all essential documents (refer to Chapter 2, "Your Essential Documents Checklist"). Love is valid; however, the law honors what's documented.

Helpful Resources:

- SSA.gov – Social Security survivor benefits

- VA.gov – Veterans Affairs survivor benefits

- Nolo.com – State-specific estate and probate laws

- WiserWomen.org – Financial planning for widows and widowers

- Employee Assistance Program (EAP) – Confidential support that some employers offer, often free, including counseling, legal or financial guidance, and help during difficult times. Contact Human Resources (HR) for details.

6.3 Losing a Parent

Handling Responsibilities with Care and Clarity

Losing a parent is deeply emotional, but legal and financial responsibilities often fall on their children. Without clear estate plans, probate can delay asset distribution, add costs, and create disputes. If minor children are involved, urgent legal action may be needed to secure their care.

How to Prepare:

- **Ensure a Will and Estate Plan Are in Place:**
  Confirm your parent has a will or living trust.
  Make sure beneficiary designations for retirement accounts, life insurance, and financial assets are updated.

- **Understand Probate:**
  Without a will, the estate must go through probate.
  Joint ownership or payable-on-death (POD) designations can help transfer assets more easily.

- **Review Debts and Financial Obligations:**
  Identify any loans, medical bills, or credit card debts.
  Children are usually not responsible unless they co-signed.

- **Plan for Minor Children (if applicable):**
  Make sure guardians are legally named in the will or guardianship documents. Without this, courts will appoint a guardian, which can delay care.

Immediate Steps After Losing a Parent:

- Obtain multiple certified copies of the death certificate.

- Notify Social Security, life insurance companies, and banks. (For help, see the ***Master List of Places to Notify After a Loved One's Passing*** in Appendix A.)

- Consult an estate attorney for probate or inheritance matters.

- Review and address any outstanding debts.

- If minor children are involved, start guardianship proceedings immediately.

Helpful Resources:

- Nolo.com – Estate planning and probate basics

- SSA.gov – Social Security survivor benefits

- LawHelp.org – Guardianship and planning for minor children

- Benefits.gov – Financial assistance after a loss

6.4 Losing a Minor Child

Facing Loss with Strength and Support

The loss of a child is one of life's greatest heartbreaks. Alongside deep grief, families often face funeral planning, medical bills, legal steps, and workplace leave during a time of shock.

How to Prepare:

- **Secure Life Insurance for Dependents:**
  While difficult to consider, life insurance for children can help cover funeral and medical expenses.

- **Understand Bereavement Leave and Workplace Protections:**
  Some employers offer paid or unpaid bereavement leave. The Family and Medical Leave Act (FMLA) may allow extended time off for grief recovery.

- **Plan for Funeral and Medical Costs:**
  Build emergency savings to prepare for unexpected expenses. Negotiate medical bills or seek help from charitable organizations if needed.

Immediate Steps After Losing a Minor Child:

- Contact your employer to arrange bereavement or FMLA leave.
- Obtain multiple certified copies of the death certificate.
- Review insurance policies for funeral or medical expense coverage.
- Seek grief counseling, support groups, or mental health services. Your job may offer free support through an Employee Assistance Program (EAP).

Helpful Resources:

- DOL.gov/FMLA – Bereavement and extended leave through FMLA
- Benefits.gov – Funeral expense assistance
- CompassionateFriends.org – Grief support for parents
- MentalHealth.gov – Mental health support resources

6.5 Losing an Adult Child

Handling Responsibilities with Strength and Compassion

Losing an adult child is life-altering. Beyond grief, families may face urgent legal and financial decisions, especially if minor children or unsettled estates are involved. Without clear plans, courts will decide custody, asset distribution, and debt management. *Please note that the preceding chapter, 'Losing a Minor Child,' contains information that may still be applicable and helpful in navigating the loss of an adult child.*

How to Prepare:

- **Confirm Guardianship Plans for Minor Children:**
  If your adult child has minor children, ensure guardianship wishes are legally documented.
  Without a plan, the court will decide custody.

- **Understand Financial Support Options for Grandchildren:**
  Explore Social Security survivor benefits.
  Consider trusts or custodial accounts to protect their financial future.

- **Review Estate and Inheritance Arrangements:**
  Confirm if your adult child has a will or named beneficiaries.
  Without clear directives, assets may go through probate.

- **Plan for Closing Personal Affairs:**
  Prepare to close accounts, settle debts, manage property, transfer vehicle titles, and notify employers and service providers. (For help, see the ***Master List of Places to Notify After a Loved One's Passing*** in Appendix A.)

Immediate Steps After Losing an Adult Child:

- Secure custody arrangements for minor children, if needed.
- Contact Social Security, insurance providers, and retirement account holders to begin survivor benefit claims.
- Consult an estate attorney to manage probate, debts, and asset transfers.
- Ensure grandchildren have access to emotional, legal, and financial support.

Helpful Resources:

- SSA.gov – Social Security survivor benefits for children
- Nolo.com – Estate planning and probate support
- LawHelp.org – Legal assistance for guardianship
- Benefits.gov – Financial planning for surviving families
- CompassionateFriends.org – Grief support for families

6.6 Losing a Sibling or Close Relative

Protecting Family Stability After Loss

Losing a sibling or close relative brings deep grief and often unexpected legal and financial responsibilities. Without an estate plan, families may face probate disputes, debt settlement challenges, and urgent custody decisions for minor children.

How to Prepare:

- **Encourage Estate Planning Early:**
  Support your sibling or close relative in creating a will or trust. Discuss who would manage their estate if needed.

- **Understand Estate and Probate Laws:**
  Without a will, the estate goes through probate under state law. Executors or administrators must settle debts, close accounts, and manage assets.

- **Plan for Minor Children (if applicable):**
  Confirm if guardianship plans are legally documented. Without them, custody decisions fall to the courts.

- **Prepare for Financial Responsibilities:**
  Most debts are paid from the estate. Surviving relatives may be responsible for co-signed debts or jointly held accounts.

Immediate Steps After Losing a Sibling or Close Relative:

- Obtain multiple certified copies of the death certificate.

- Locate and review any wills, trusts, or estate plans.

- Notify creditors, financial institutions, and service providers. (For help, see the ***Master List of Places to Notify After a Loved One's Passing*** in Appendix A.)

- If minor children are involved, initiate guardianship proceedings with legal support.

Helpful Resources:

- Nolo.com – Estate planning and probate basics
- LawHelp.org – Guardianship for minor children
- ConsumerFinance.gov – Debt settlement guidance
- CompassionateFriends.org – Grief support and family counseling

CHAPTER 7

Financial Disruptions

Navigating Financial Change with Clarity

Life events like job loss, divorce, injury, or housing instability can shake your financial foundation. This chapter offers clear, practical steps to protect your essential needs and make strong, steady decisions during uncertain times.

Topics Covered:

- Managing Job Loss or Sudden Income Disruption
- Navigating Divorce or Separation
- Injured on the Job: Understanding Your Rights
- Facing Housing Instability or Foreclosure

7.1 Managing Job Loss or Sudden Income Disruption

Protecting Your Stability During Transition

Sudden job loss can create a financial crisis and emotional strain. With many Americans living paycheck to paycheck, even a short income gap can lead to hardship. Swift action and proactive planning can help you recover stronger.

How to Prepare:

- **Build an Emergency Fund:**
  Save 3–6 months of living expenses in a high-yield savings account. Automate small contributions to grow the amount steadily.

- **Know Your Legal Rights and Severance Benefits:**
  Negotiate severance pay if laid off. Review COBRA options and apply for unemployment immediately.
  Check for WARN Act protections.

- **Stay Job-Ready:**
  Keep your resume, LinkedIn profile, and references updated. Maintain strong professional connections.

- **Diversify Income Streams:**
  Explore side hustles, freelance work, or gig economy jobs to supplement income.

Immediate Steps After Job Loss:

- Apply for unemployment benefits through your state's Department of Labor.

- Prioritize essential expenses: housing, utilities, food, and health insurance.

- Explore short-term income opportunities like contract work or freelancing.
- Secure continued health coverage through COBRA, the ACA Marketplace, or Medicaid.

Common Challenges and Solutions:

- **Delayed Unemployment Benefits:**
  Apply immediately and use emergency savings if available.

- **Difficulty Finding a New Job:**
  Expand your search to remote roles, contract work, or new industries. Consider short-term training to upskill.

- **Emotional and Mental Strain:**
  Maintain a structured routine.
  Seek career counseling and access mental health support if needed.

Final Empowerment Note:

Job loss does not define your future.
By acting swiftly, protecting your finances, and staying open to new opportunities, you can rebuild with resilience and confidence.

Helpful Resources:

- CareerOneStop.org – Unemployment benefits and job search support
- DOL.gov/COBRA – Health coverage options
- Benefits.gov – Rental assistance programs
- CareerOneStop.org – Career counseling and short-term training
- MentalHealth.gov – Mental health support resources

7.2 Navigating Divorce or Separation

Protecting Your Future Through Transition

Divorce impacts emotional well-being, financial security, and legal standing. Without preparation, it can create long-term hardship. Strategic planning protects your rights, assets, and future stability.

How to Prepare:

- **Seek Legal Counsel Early:**
  Consult a family law attorney to understand your rights and state-specific laws.

- **Organize Finances:**
  Gather tax returns, bank statements, property records, and retirement account details.

- **Separate Financial Accounts:**
  Open individual accounts, establish separate credit, and close or freeze joint accounts.

- **Prioritize Custody and Child Support Planning:**
  Create enforceable custody and support agreements focused on the child's well-being.

Immediate Steps After Divorce or Separation:

After your divorce or separation is finalized, take steps to protect your next chapter:

- Update legal documents (will, power of attorney, healthcare proxy)
- Change beneficiaries on insurance, retirement, and financial accounts
- Secure housing and utilities in your name only

- Check and rebuild your credit if needed
- Consult a tax professional about your new filing status
- Notify key institutions (employer, banks, insurers) of your updated status
- Ensure custody and support agreements are legally documented

Common Challenges and Solutions:

- **Emotional Decision-Making:**
  Work with legal, financial, and counseling professionals rather than making emotional choices.
- **Hidden Assets and Debts:**
  Hire a forensic accountant if needed.
- **Child Support and Alimony Disputes:**
  Use mediation or legal representation to secure fair agreements.

Final Empowerment Note:

Divorce, while painful, can be a turning point toward renewed independence and security. By preparing financially, protecting your rights, and building emotional support, you can move forward with dignity and resilience.

Helpful Resources:

- APA.org – Divorce statistics and emotional health
- NBER.org – Post-divorce income study
- Census.gov – Child support and custody data
- Nolo.com – Divorce legal guides
- WIFE.org – Financial planning for women after divorce

7.3 Injured on the Job? Understanding Your Rights

Protecting Your Health, Income, and Legal Rights

Workplace injuries can bring medical costs, lost wages, and long-term challenges. While workers' compensation laws exist to protect employees, many face claim denials, retaliation, or pressure to return before fully healing. Understanding your rights and acting quickly helps secure fair treatment and financial support.

Immediate Steps After a Workplace Injury:

If you're hurt on the job, take these steps right away to protect your health, income, and rights:

- **Report the injury immediately.**
  Notify your supervisor and complete an incident report. Delays can hurt your claim.

- **Get medical care from an approved provider.**
  Follow all treatment instructions and ensure every injury is documented.

- **File a workers' comp claim promptly.**
  Each state has deadlines. Filing ensures access to medical care and wage support.

- **Keep detailed records.**
  Save reports, doctor's notes, and all communication related to your injury.

- **Track your claim.**
  Appeal if denied, and consider consulting a workers' comp attorney.

- **Watch for retaliation.**
  You're legally protected. Report issues to OSHA, your state labor board, or the EEOC.

- **Don't rush back to work.**
  Return only with full medical clearance. You have the right to heal fully.

Final Empowerment Note:

A workplace injury does not strip you of your rights.
By acting swiftly, securing proper care, and standing firm, you protect your health, your recovery, and your future.

Helpful Resources:

- BLS.gov – Workplace injury data
- OSHA.gov – Occupational Safety and Health Administration
- EEOC.gov – Worker protections under EEOC
- NELP.org – National Employment Law Project
- USA.gov – State workers' compensation boards
- Injured Workers' Groups – Workers' compensation advocacy

7.4 Facing Housing Instability or Foreclosure

Taking Action to Protect Your Stability

Housing instability can result from job loss, medical debt, rising interest rates, or unexpected hardship. Without early action, foreclosure or eviction can damage credit, disrupt family life, and delay financial recovery. Knowing your rights and relief options helps protect your home and future.

How to Protect Yourself from Housing Loss:

If you're falling behind on rent or mortgage payments, don't wait—early action can prevent long-term damage. These steps can help you stay housed and preserve your financial stability:

- **Communicate with your lender or landlord immediately.**
  Ask about deferments, payment plans, or hardship relief. The earlier you reach out, the more options you have.

- **Explore mortgage and rental assistance programs.**
  Federal, state, and nonprofit resources offer forbearance, rental aid, and emergency housing support.

- **Know your legal rights.**
  Evictions and foreclosures must follow strict legal procedures. Learn your rights under local and federal housing laws.

- **Apply for housing support through HUD or trusted agencies.**
  Seek help from HUD-certified counselors or local nonprofits. Many offer free assistance with applications and legal navigation.

- **Protect yourself from scams.**
  Avoid "fast fix" offers. Always verify organizations through HUD.gov or local housing authorities.

- **Create a personal recovery plan.**
  Include temporary housing options, legal aid, financial counseling, and credit repair steps to restore long-term stability.

Final Empowerment Note:

Housing instability is frightening, but you are not powerless. By acting early, knowing your rights, and using available resources, you can protect your home and rebuild your stability.

Helpful Resources:

- ConsumerFinance.gov – Foreclosure resources
- HUD.gov – Housing assistance and resources
- EvictionLab.org – U.S. eviction and housing reports
- FHFA.gov – Mortgage relief options
- HUD.gov/Counselors – HUD-certified housing counselors
- NLIHC.org – Emergency housing resources
- 211.org – Local housing assistance
- FindLegalAid.org – Tenant and homeowner legal support

CHAPTER 8

Military & Service-Related Events

Preparing for Deployments and Service Changes

Military service brings unique responsibilities and sacrifices. This chapter offers practical steps to prepare financially, legally, and emotionally for deployments, activations, and service transitions. Planning ahead protects your security and brings peace of mind to you and your loved ones.

8.1 Military Deployment or Active-Duty Service

Preparing Your Life with Love and Readiness

Deployment often comes with little warning and long separations. Having key legal, financial, and caregiving documents ready protects your family, home, and personal affairs while you serve. Preparation brings peace of mind to both service members and their loved ones.

8.2 Deployment Readiness Checklist

Important Documents to Prepare Before Active-Duty Service

Legal and Financial Essentials:

- General and specific powers of attorney
- Will, living will, and medical power of attorney
- Updated beneficiary designations (life insurance, pensions, retirement accounts)
- Guardianship documents for minor children or dependents
- List of bank accounts, insurance policies, and investment

accounts

- Online access instructions (banking, bill payments, passwords)

Home, Property, and Personal Matters:

- Deed or lease information
- Homeowners or renters insurance policies
- Vehicle titles, registrations, and insurance
- Property maintenance and utility plans

Family and Emergency Contacts:

- Emergency contact list (family, attorney, doctor, POA agent)
- Childcare or pet care instructions
- Military support contacts (Family Readiness Officer, Legal Aid Office)

Sharing Important Documents with a Trusted Person:

It's crucial to ensure a trusted individual has access to secure copies (physical or digital) of your important documents for emergencies. Here's a list of items to share:

- Passport and identification documents
- Social Security card and military service records
- Deployment orders (copy to trusted family or legal representative)
- Safe deposit box location and key (if applicable)

By preparing these secure copies in advance, you can provide peace of mind for yourself and your trusted person during unforeseen circumstances.

8.3 Helpful Resources for Military & Service-Related Preparation

Use these trusted resources to take the next step in organizing your affairs, protecting your loved ones, and accessing the benefits you've earned through service.

Legal and Financial Support

- **Military OneSource – Legal & Financial Assistance**
  A free resource for active-duty, National Guard, and Reserve members and their families. Offers legal document templates, financial counseling, and deployment checklists.
  Website: militaryonesource.mil

- **Servicemembers Civil Relief Act (SCRA)**
  Provides legal protections for active-duty military members, including relief from certain financial and housing obligations during service.
  Website: justice.gov/servicemembers

- **Military Legal Assistance Office Locator**
  Find a free legal office on base to help with powers of attorney, wills, and family legal planning.
  Website: legalassistance.law.af.mil

Emergency and Family Readiness

- **Family Readiness System (FRS)**
  Offers emotional and logistical support for service members and their families, including relocation assistance and family care planning.
  Website: militaryonesource.mil/family-relationships

- **National Military Family Association (NMFA)**
  Advocacy and education for military families. Offers programs for caregivers, children, and spouses during deployments and transitions.
  Website: militaryfamily.org

Document and Benefits Access

- **Defense Finance and Accounting Service (DFAS)**
  Manage your military pay, retirement accounts, and survivor benefit plans.
  Website: dfas.mil

- **VA Benefits – U.S. Department of Veterans Affairs**
  Apply for service-connected benefits, health care, and burial planning.
  Website: va.gov

- **eBenefits Portal**
  Access your personal military records, insurance, and discharge paperwork.
  Website: ebenefits.va.gov

Proactive Planning Tools

- **Military OneSource's Deployment Checklist**
  Step-by-step guide to help you prepare for activation or deployment.
  Website: militaryonesource.mil

- **Veterans Affairs Advance Directive Tool**
  Helps you complete a legally valid advance directive and name a health care agent.
  Website: va.gov/geriatrics

Tip:

Even if you're not deploying, creating a Family Emergency Binder with these documents prepares your loved ones for any unexpected event. Bookmark these resources or add them to your binder for quick access, and keep completed forms with your ICE Plan or share them with a trusted contact.

Final Encouragement:

You don't have to complete everything at once.
Every document you gather strengthens your foundation.
Your preparation is a powerful act of love for your family, your future, and the life you're building beyond this moment.

CHAPTER 9

Natural Disasters and Emergency Preparedness

Building Readiness: Protecting Your Family and Finances

Natural disasters can strike without warning, causing displacement, financial loss, and emotional strain. In 2023 alone, FEMA recorded 25 billion-dollar disasters across the U.S.

This chapter offers practical steps to help you prepare for natural disasters, protect your loved ones, and recover with greater ease—physically, financially, and emotionally.

While disasters are unpredictable, preparation protects your family, finances, and peace of mind.

Having an emergency plan, knowing how to file insurance claims, and understanding available aid can speed recovery and reduce stress.

Key Considerations: The Real-World Impact of Disasters

Financial Losses and Insurance Gaps:
Many homeowners and renters are underinsured without realizing it.

Displacement and Housing Insecurity:
Stable housing can be difficult to secure after disasters.

Emergency Aid and Relief Delays:
FEMA aid and insurance claims often take weeks or months.

Business and Employment Disruptions:
Small businesses often struggle to recover without a contingency plan.

Health and Safety Risks:
Poor preparation can cause food shortages, medical emergencies, and loss of essential services.

9.1 Best Practices for Disaster Readiness

- Create a disaster kit: food, water, medications, flashlights, batteries, first aid, and important documents.
- Review and update insurance annually.
- Develop an evacuation and communication plan.
- Store key documents in a fireproof, waterproof safe.
- Learn about FEMA, the Red Cross, and local aid programs.
- Back up digital records securely.

9.2 Common Challenges and Solutions

- **Delayed Insurance Payouts:**
  Document damage thoroughly and track all communications with insurers.

- **Insufficient Emergency Savings:**
  Build a dedicated emergency fund and explore disaster grants and loans.

- **Limited Awareness of Aid Programs:**
  Pre-register with FEMA and research local support resources.

- **Power Outages and Communication Failures:**
  Use solar-powered radios, emergency chargers, and pre-set family meeting points.

9.3 Helpful Resources

When disaster strikes, these trusted sources offer guidance, support, and recovery assistance:

- FEMA.gov – Federal disaster aid, emergency alerts, and recovery assistance.

- Ready.gov – Emergency planning tools, evacuation guides, and checklists.

- RedCross.org – Shelter locations, disaster relief, and family preparedness tips.

- DisasterAssistance.gov – Central site to apply for and track federal disaster aid.

- NOAA.gov – Weather alerts, storm updates, and climate risk information.

- HUD.gov – Housing support, relocation help, and disaster recovery programs.

- SBA.gov – Disaster loans for homeowners, renters, and small businesses.

- InsuranceInformationInstitute.org – Info on insurance coverage, claims, and disaster protection.

- SalvationArmyUSA.org – Emergency food, shelter, and financial assistance.

- 211.org – Local help with shelters, food, mental health, and disaster resources.

- Rescue.org – Disaster recovery and planning resources for vulnerable communities.

- CDC.gov – Public health guidance for disasters, evacuations, and water safety.

CHAPTER 10

Your Next Steps

Staying Ready for Life's Changes

You've made it to the final chapter, and that's no small thing.

Taking the time to plan, gather documents, and speak with loved ones is a powerful act of care.

But preparedness isn't a one-time project.

It's a living, breathing practice that grows with you as life evolves.

The goal isn't perfection.

The goal is peace of mind.

This chapter will show you how to keep your plan up to date, recognize when changes are needed, and stay grounded no matter what life brings.

10.1 Maintain Your Plan Over Time

Life moves fast.

Births, deaths, marriages, relocations, and career shifts—each one can affect your plans and priorities.

That's why your preparedness plan should stay active, not tucked away and forgotten.

Make it a habit to review your plan once a year.

Choose a meaningful date: your birthday, New Year's Day, or tax season. Even 15 minutes can keep you ahead of the unexpected.

What to Review Each Year:

- Are all contact details (doctors, lawyers, emergency contacts) current?

- Any updates in health, insurance, or benefits?

- Are your beneficiaries still accurate?

- Has your marital, financial, or household status changed?

- Do your documents still reflect your wishes and values?

10.2 Update Documents After Major Life Events

Some events call for immediate updates—not just emotionally, but legally and financially. These moments are your signal to revisit your documents:

- Birth or adoption

- Marriage, divorce, or partnership changes

- Death of a loved one listed in your documents

- Major medical diagnoses or surgeries

- Changes in finances (new job, retirement, inheritance, or debt)

- A move, especially to assisted living or long-term care

Quick Tip:

After a major event, set a phone reminder to review your documents within 30 days. You don't need to update everything at once—just take one step.

10.3 Why Printed Emergency Information Is Non-Negotiable

Technology is convenient, but it's not always reliable when it matters most.

Phone batteries die.
Wi-Fi fails.
Passwords get forgotten.
Cloud systems go offline.

In emergencies, printed information can mean the difference between swift action and costly delays.

Real-Life Examples:

- **FEMA delays:** Many families can't prove who they are or where they lived without paper documentation.

- **Medication access:** If pharmacy systems go down, a printed list of medications could save your life.

- **Banking freezes:** Without digital access, printed contact info and account summaries help speed up recovery.

What to Print

You don't need to print everything—just the essentials:

- Copies of ID cards (driver's license, passport, Social Security card)

- Health insurance cards and a current medication list

- Emergency contacts and medical directives

- Powers of attorney and advance care documents

- A summary of life insurance and key accounts

- Property deeds or lease agreements

- Bank and insurance provider contact numbers
- A secure, printed password list (stored carefully)

Tip: Review and refresh these documents yearly or after major life changes.

How to Store Printed Documents Safely

- Use a clearly labeled emergency folder
- Store it in a fireproof, water-resistant document bag
- Keep it in a secure but accessible location
- Tell a trusted loved one where it's kept, especially if you live alone

10.4 Gentle Reminder: Use Both Digital and Physical Tools

You don't have to choose—your strength is in the combination.

Let digital tools support your everyday ease.
Let printed backups safeguard your peace of mind.

Think of your emergency folder as a gift to your future self—and to the people who love you.
Taking this small step today can prevent big stress tomorrow.

10.5 Stay Empowered: Progress, Not Perfection

Maybe you didn't complete every document.
Maybe there are still conversations to have.
That's okay. You're not behind; you're in motion.
Preparedness isn't about doing it all at once.
It's about building momentum, one intentional step at a time.

Every page you read, every form you filled out, and every conversation you initiated are acts of love. They are signs of leadership.

If you ever feel overwhelmed, remember:

- You don't need to be perfect to be protected.

- You can always return to this work when you're ready.

- Every effort you make today protects your peace tomorrow.

10.6 Final Words of Encouragement

You began this journey to protect what matters most: yourself, your loved ones, and your peace of mind. And you've done exactly that.

Keep going.
Keep evolving.
Keep your plan within reach.

Life will always bring the unexpected, but now you have the wisdom, tools, and confidence to meet it with grace and power.

This guide will be here when you need to revisit it.

Every step you take from here is another act of preparation, empowerment, and love.

You are ready.
Stay ready.

Thank You for Your Support

It has been an honor to share these insights with you. If this book has inspired or guided you, your review would mean the world, helping others discover this message and join the journey.

If you're interested in having Maria give a transformational keynote talk or discuss other opportunities, please email **contact@mariasturner.com**. Thank you for being a part of this journey.

APPENDICES

Appendix A: Master List of Places to Notify After a Loved One's Passing

💼 Financial Institutions

- Banks (checking, savings, CDs, safe deposit boxes)
- Credit card companies (including store cards like Macy's, Lowe's, etc.)
- Mortgage company or lender
- Auto loan lender
- Investment accounts (Fidelity, Charles Schwab, etc.)
- Retirement accounts (401(k), IRA, pensions)

🏛️Government Agencies

- Social Security Administration (even if they weren't receiving benefits)
- Internal Revenue Service (IRS) (final tax returns will be required)
- Department of Veterans Affairs (VA) (if military service is involved)
- State Department of Revenue (for state taxes, if applicable)
- Local election board (to cancel voter registration)
- Passport agency (submit passport for cancellation)

🚗 Vehicle and Property

- Department of Motor Vehicles (DMV) – to cancel driver's license and transfer titles

- Auto insurance company
- Homeowners or renters insurance
- Property management company or landlord (if they were renting)

⊕ Healthcare and Benefits

- Health insurance provider (private insurance, Medicare, Medicaid)
- Dental and vision insurance
- Pharmacy or mail-order prescriptions
- Long-term care insurance provider
- Disability insurance provider
- Employer benefits department (if applicable)

📝 Legal and Professional

- Attorney (if they had one regarding estate matters, wills, trusts, etc.)
- Accountant or tax preparer
- Financial advisor
- Insurance agents (life insurance, annuities)

▯ Utilities and Household Services

- Electric company
- Gas company
- Water and sewer
- Trash collection
- Internet and cable providers
- Cell phone carrier

- Home security services
- Subscription services (Amazon Prime, Netflix, magazines)

📫 Mail and Deliveries

- United States Postal Service (forward or hold mail)
- UPS, FedEx, Amazon (if deliveries were set up)

📚 Memberships and Associations

- Professional organizations (Bar Association, Alumni Groups, Trade Unions)
- Religious or spiritual organizations (churches, temples, mosques)
- Clubs or memberships (gym, country clubs, libraries)

❤ Personal Accounts

- Email providers (Gmail, Yahoo, Outlook)
- Social media accounts (Facebook, Instagram, LinkedIn, etc.)
- Online shopping accounts (Amazon, Etsy, PayPal, eBay)
- Streaming services (Netflix, Spotify, Audible)

✦ Gentle Tips:

- **Start with Social Security.** This triggers many automatic processes, including canceling Medicare if they had it.
- **Order multiple certified copies** of the death certificate (typically 5–10). Most institutions will require an official copy, not a photocopy.
- **Keep a master log** of who you contacted and when, and make notes about any next steps they require.
- **Request final bills in writing** and keep copies for your records.

- **Pause subscriptions** and unnecessary services early to avoid fees stacking up.

Appendix B: Soft Timeline for Managing Affairs After a Loss

First 24 – 48 Hours: Immediate and Urgent Steps

- Notify hospice, hospital, or authorities to officially pronounce death.
- Arrange transport of the body (contact a funeral home or cremation service).
- Notify immediate family and key contacts.
- Secure their home, vehicles, and valuables.
- Ensure care for dependents and pets.

First 7 Days: Important Early Actions

- Obtain multiple certified copies of the death certificate.
- Confirm funeral, memorial, or celebration of life plans.
- Locate important documents (will, insurance policies, financial records).
- Notify their employer and inquire about benefits or final paycheck.
- Contact Social Security Administration and applicable benefits offices.

Weeks 2 – 4: Building the Foundation

- Set up an estate management system (binder, folder, or digital tracker).
- Begin probate process if needed (file the will or initiate estate court proceedings).

- Begin closing or transferring financial accounts.

- Update or forward mail through USPS.

- Cancel or pause subscriptions, utilities, and memberships in the deceased's name.

- Begin sorting through property and belongings at your own pace.

Weeks 5 – 6: Completing Key Transitions

- Identify and address outstanding debts and financial obligations.

- File final income tax return (Form 1040 and/or Form 1041 if estate income applies).

- Consider planning an extended memorial tribute or charitable donation in their name (optional).

- Update your own will, beneficiaries, healthcare proxy, and emergency plans.

Gentle Reminders Throughout

- Give yourself permission to move at the speed of your healing, not external expectations.

- Rest when needed; grief is physical, mental, emotional, and spiritual.

- Celebrate every completed task, no matter how small. You are doing sacred work.

- Ask for help when needed—legal, financial, emotional, or spiritual.

Appendix C: Master Checklist: Essential Documents Overview

Identity & Personal Records (for you and all dependents)

- Birth Certificates
- Social Security Cards
- Government-Issued IDs (passports, driver's licenses, state IDs)
- Citizenship or Immigration Papers (Green Card, Naturalization Certificate)
- Name Change Documents (if applicable)

Marital & Family Documents

- Marriage Certificate
- Divorce Decree/Separation Agreement
- Prenuptial/Postnuptial Agreement (if applicable)
- Adoption Records
- Custody Agreements and Child Support Orders
- Legal Guardianship Documents

Property & Real Estate Documents

- Property Deeds and Titles (homes, land, vehicles)
- Mortgage Documents and Loan Agreements
- Lease or Rental Agreements
- Property Tax Records
- Homeowners or Renters Insurance Policy

Financial Records

- Tax Returns (last 3–5 years)
- Bank Statements (checking, savings, joint accounts)
- Investment and Retirement Account Statements (stocks, bonds, IRAs, 401(k)s, annuities)
- Credit Card Statements
- Loan Agreements and Promissory Notes (student loans, personal loans, business loans)
- Pay Stubs/Income Verification (for self-employed individuals)

Insurance Policies

- Life Insurance Policy (with updated beneficiaries)
- Health Insurance Policy and Card (including dental and vision)
- Disability Insurance Policy (short-term and long-term coverage)
- Long-Term Care Insurance Policy
- Auto Insurance Policy
- Homeowners or Renters Insurance Policy
- Umbrella Insurance Policy

Estate Planning Documents

- Last Will and Testament
- Codicils (legal amendments to a will)
- Trust Documents (revocable or irrevocable)
- Power of Attorney (for Financial and Legal Affairs)
- Medical Power of Attorney (Healthcare Proxy)

- Living Will / Advance Healthcare Directive
- Beneficiary Designation Forms (life insurance, retirement accounts)
- Letter of Instruction (funeral wishes, obituary details, account information, personal notes)

Business Documents (If Applicable)

- Business Formation Documents (LLC, Corporation, Sole Proprietorship)
- Business Licenses and Permits
- Partnership or Operating Agreements
- Business Insurance Policies
- Succession Plan

Additional Important Records

- Educational Records and Diplomas
- Medical and Immunization Records (including family medical history)
- Vehicle Titles and Registrations
- Receipts for Major Purchases (jewelry, electronics, art, furniture, etc.)
- Charitable Contribution Records
- Safe Deposit Box Inventory
- Digital Asset Information (email, social media, cryptocurrency, online banking access)

Appendix D: Quick Digital Inventory Template

Use this template to record and organize your essential digital assets. Store a copy in your Emergency Binder or a secure digital vault. Review and update it annually.

1. Password Manager
- Name of service or app:
- Master password location:
- Emergency access instructions:

2. Financial Accounts
(Include login usernames and note where passwords are stored securely.)
- Bank(s):
- Credit union(s):
- Investment accounts:
- Retirement accounts:
- Crypto wallets or apps:
- Payment apps (e.g., PayPal, Venmo):

3. Communication & Media
- Primary email:
- Backup/recovery email:
- Social media accounts:
  - o Facebook:
  - o Instagram:
  - o Other:
- Cloud storage (e.g., Google Drive, Dropbox, iCloud):
  - o Service name:
  - o Login/password storage location:

4. *Business & Creative Assets*
- Website/domain names:
- Hosting provider:
- Online store(s) or platforms:
- Client databases, digital products, or intellectual property:

5. *Devices*
(List device names and associated access codes/passwords.)
- Phone unlock code:
- Laptop password:
- Tablet password:
- External hard drive details:

6. *Subscription Services*
(List recurring monthly or annual subscriptions.)
- Streaming (e.g., Netflix, Spotify):
- Shopping/memberships (e.g., Amazon, Costco):
- Software (e.g., Microsoft, Canva, Adobe):
- Other:

7. *Legacy Instructions*
- Legacy contact for social media accounts:
- Digital trustee (name and contact information):
- Location of this completed document:

Signature & Date of Last Review
- Signed:
- Date:

Appendix E: Conversation Starters for Chapter 4: Communicating with Loved Ones

Use these gentle questions to open meaningful dialogue and invite shared preparedness with calmness, care, and compassion.

Hospital/ICE Plan/Emergency Binder

1. Have you written down your emergency contacts or healthcare wishes yet?

2. If something unexpected happened, would your loved ones know where to find your important documents?

3. Have you named someone to speak on your behalf during a medical emergency?

4. Do you have an ICE (In Case of Emergency) contact saved in your phone?

5. Would you like me to help you put together an emergency binder or checklist?

Talking with Aging Parents or Elders

6. Have you thought about what kind of care you'd want if you were hospitalized and couldn't speak for yourself?

7. Is there someone you trust to manage your affairs if something were to happen to you?

8. Do you have a will, an advance directive, or a power of attorney in place?

Talking with Adult Children or Younger Family Members

9. Do you know where our family's important documents are kept in case you ever need them?

10. Would you feel comfortable telling me your preferences if you ever needed emergency care?

11. Do you want help getting your own plan started so you're protected too?

General Family Conversations

12. Have we talked about who we would each call first in an emergency?

13. Would you feel better knowing where my emergency information is kept?

14. Is there anything you've always wanted to put in writing but haven't yet?

15. Do you want to have a family check-in about our plans and contacts, just so we're all on the same page?

Appendix F: Helpful Programs to Know About

A High-Level Resource List for Navigating Life's Unexpected Moments

These programs offer foundational support for individuals and families navigating medical emergencies, caregiving transitions, financial hardships, or unexpected loss. Use the keywords listed to search for localized options in your city or state.

1. Financial Assistance & Income Support

- **Social Security Survivor Benefits**
  For surviving spouses and dependents. Visit: ssa.gov
  Search keywords: "Social Security benefits after death"

- **Temporary Assistance for Needy Families (TANF)**
  Monthly financial support for low-income families.
  Keywords: "TANF + [Your State]"

- **Low-Income Home Energy Assistance Program (LIHEAP)**
  Utility assistance for eligible households.
  Keywords: "LIHEAP application + [Your State]"

- **Unemployment Insurance (UI)**
  Financial aid for job loss.
  Keywords: "Apply for unemployment + [Your State]"

2. Meal & Grocery Delivery Services

- **Meals on Wheels America**
  Hot meal delivery for seniors or those homebound.
  Visit: mealsonwheelsamerica.org

- **Supplemental Nutrition Assistance Program (SNAP)**
  Monthly grocery benefit for eligible individuals.
  Keywords: "Apply for SNAP + [Your State]"

- **Local Food Banks / Pantries**
  Locate food resources via feedingamerica.org
  Keywords: "Emergency food assistance + [City]"

3. Caregiver, Elder & Disability Support

- **Area Agencies on Aging (AAA)**
  Resources for elder care, caregiver relief, and in-home support.
  Visit: eldercare.acl.gov

- **Medicaid Home & Community-Based Services (HCBS)**
  State-run programs for assisted living or in-home care.
  Keywords: "HCBS waiver + [Your State]"

- **National Alliance for Caregiving**
  Research, advocacy, and caregiver tools.
  Visit: caregiving.org

- **State Departments of Disability Services**
  Services for those living with disabilities.
  Keywords: "Disability services + [Your State]"

4. Burial & End-of-Life Assistance

- **State Funeral Assistance Programs**
  May cover basic cremation or burial expenses.
  Keywords: "Funeral assistance + [Your State]"

- **Veterans Affairs (VA) Burial Benefits**
  Honors, reimbursements, and plot support.
  Visit: va.gov/burials-memorials

- **Final Expense / Burial Insurance**
  Financial support for funerals and estate closure.
  Keywords: "Final expense life insurance claim process"

5. Emotional & Mental Health Support

- **211 by United Way**
  National 24/7 referral line for grief support, therapy, and basic needs.
  Call: 2-1-1 or visit 211.org

- **GriefShare**
  Free or low-cost local grief recovery groups.
  Visit: griefshare.org

- **Sliding Scale Counseling Services**
  Mental health providers who offer reduced rates based on income.
  Keywords: "Sliding scale therapist + [City]"

6. Legal Aid & Advocacy Services

- **Legal Aid Societies**
  Free or low-cost legal support for civil matters such as housing, benefits, or custody.
  Keywords: "Legal Aid + [Your City or State]"
  Example: Legal Aid Society of NYC, Atlanta Legal Aid, Bay Area Legal Aid

- **LawHelp.org**
  National directory of legal aid programs by topic and state.
  Visit: lawhelp.org

- **Elder Law Attorneys**
  Specialists in estate, guardianship, POA, and elder care planning.
  Keywords: "Elder law attorney + [Your City]"

- **National Center on Law & Elder Rights (NCLER)**
  Tools for elder legal support and professional advocates.
  Visit: ncler.acl.gov

- **State Bar Referral Services**
  Match with vetted attorneys through your local bar association.
  Keywords: "Lawyer referral + [Your State]"

7. Support Through Your Employer

- **Employee Assistance Program (EAP)**
  Confidential services some employers offer, including counseling, legal and financial guidance, and crisis support, often at no cost.
  Keywords: "Employee Assistance Program + [Your Employer]" or contact your HR department directly

www.ingramcontent.com/pod-product-compliance
Lightning Source LLC
Chambersburg PA
CBHW061658120626
46550CB00003B/990